English translation by Geraldine Braithwaite
and Massimo Carlucci

VENICE

Giancarlo Gasponi

VENICE

Artistic Collaboration
Rouhyeh Avaregan

Introduction
Carlo Sgorlon

Text by
Tiziano Rizzo

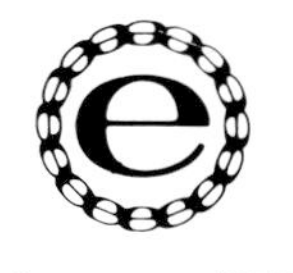

Editoria - Trento

Carlo Sgorlon

The faces of Venice

Venice lives in the imagination of everyone even long before they have a chance of seeing it, and there is barely an inhabitant on this earth with even the minimum of culture for whom this name does not conjure up a wide range of sensations and images. Venice, even before being a city, — perhaps the most beautiful and unique in the world — is the central point of a halo of myths and reverberations which radiate outwards like ripples in the water when a stone is dropped into it. The nearer you get to the heart which emanates and diffuses it, the more intense the halo becomes. In the Venetian territories, like Friuli, where I live, which belonged to the Serenissima for more than three centuries, one can perceive everywhere the fascination irradiated by Venice. For centuries the Friulan peasant cherished the dream of going there, of seeing the capital, imagined like a kind of magical place or Paradise. He would even break, for once in his life, the iron rule of frugality imposed on him by necessity, to bring to life, among the little streets and alleyways and canals of Venice, the full extent of his wonder and admiration.
Usually this would happen on his honeymoon. Among its hundreds of singular characteristics, Venice possesses this also, of being a nuptial city, where one goes because its scenario, as though in a fantastic theatre, may be the background of conjugal sweetness and joy. There was, and perhaps there is still, a popular Friulan saying which throws light on it. "Viodi Vignesie" or "to see Venice", in my childhood meant to steal a glance at an intimate moment of a beautiful young girl. There was, then, a strong link between the city of the Doges and the hidden attractions of woman and of love. If Venice was the city of love for great writers such as D'Annunzio (*The Fire*), of Bacchelli (*The City of Lovers*), the same thing could have happened to the simple spirits from the Venetian domain. But can Venice, the mirage city, the dream city which evokes infinite images, live up to all her promises?
She did for me. I saw her for the first time at the age of seventeen when I was in my last year at school. I went

there with my school to visit the Biennale, in which there were also paintings of the Impressionist and the Romantic eras. I saw, then, some of the great oil paintings of Turner with their blurred atmosphere dissolving into light. Venice seemed to me a Turneresque city.
I saw it wrapped in mist, bathed in the golden glow of a twilight slowly clouding over. The houses, bridges, and the waters of the canals were vanishing into the soft, rich light glazed over by a light fog, fading into an almost unreal atmosphere rich in painterly touches. I saw Venice many other times and often the city showed me the image which had so impressed me on my first encounter. When she seems to melt and dissolve into twilight... Venice shows one of her most authentic faces; that of an improbable city, of a fantastic and shimmering mirage, a vision created by the colourful and magic atmosphere of the lagoon. Perhaps, above all, the Venice of Diego Valeri, who was one of her most enamoured and faithful poets. Venice, with her barely sketched islands, with outlines fused into a single colour between mauve and grey, and in the sleepy sunset of the lagoon, seems indeed a city created by a unique gift of the gods. A city you have to gaze at, imprint on your memory because perhaps it is destined to disappear in the dissolution of a certain condition of air and light; a phantom city, a metaphor for the transient quality of life and the works of man which now are, but soon will disappear, swallowed up by the dark vortex of the past.
But even when it shows all the consistence of a city of bricks and stones, Venice is never completely free of her character of a place standing outside time, apart from, and impervious to, so many characteristics of our age; the constant rush, the rapidity of travel, the fervour to produce, the anxiety to succeed and to use one's own time well. Venice is the city where all the rhythms are slowed down by necessity by her very nature. The visitor who arrives there must leave his means of transport at Piazzale Roma together with his sense of rush. One does not go to Venice to deal with business and make money with one's time. Its little nineteenth-century water buses,

its motor boats, a little more modern, and boats with outboard motors move slowly along the green water lanes without forcing the placid, wise and contemplative rhythm of the city. Not to mention the gondolas which still move with the speed of when Venice was the Queen of the seas. The city, in a certain way imposes the same slow pace in all her veins and arteries with the same ease, whether of water or of stones. Therefore, this famous line, "Avanti, pian, quasi indrio" (slowly forward, almost backwards), seems to me a kind of motto typically hers, a sort of emblem. In Venice you are compelled to free yourself from the oppressive idea that time flies, and to assume through necessity the same philosophy as the Venetian who lets it pass by with a sly smile, a little sceptical and ironic, with the attitude of one who knows that to follow it panting is, after all, a curse.

In Venice, while walking through the crowd made up of tourists from the five continents, there arise in us again lost pleasures. The enjoyment of being with others, to mingle with the crowd, to stroll about forgetting for a while that we have invented a number of means for hurriedly travelling between one tormented spot and another on our planet. Moving about in the city of the Doges on foot or in the waterboats, means that you are continually immersed in the crowd. Venice is not only an island in space, a splendid city shaped like a shell: but it is also isolated in time, a space where speed seems to have been banished to an exile far away. In Venice one almost forgets to belong to the age of anxiety and rush. One rediscovers in depth one's own contemplative dimension, because Venice is a city to enjoy visually, yet to appreciate with the five senses, of which sight takes the lion's share. Wherever it turns, it lights upon a masterpiece. It undergoes a sort of continuous assault by beautiful things for which it begs almost to rest, to turn to something grey and indifferent. Even the thousands of antique and bric-a-brac shops in Venice, can be a diversion, something more trivial to look at, so as not to clutter up the mind with overwhelming images which it can no longer select and put in their proper place. Another agreeable characteristic of Venice is that of chatting to people, that is, "ciacolar". Venice is one of those happy 'drawing-room' cities left in the world, that is the city in which such a quality is still most in evidence. Venice has always been a city cut out for the chance meeting and the affable exchange, because the little squares and alleys, the covered passages, the bridges, the quaint asymmetrical steps, all born under the influence of a fantastic geometry, playfully deceptive, are only the extension of the house, the breakfast room, the kitchen or the coffee shop.

In Venice the life and vitality of the streets are, perhaps, more light-hearted and appealing than that of the indoors. Every stone, every capital, every well, every architrave, every church square has an atmosphere, affable and homely which makes conversation and human interchange easier. It is natural to talk to someone who appears at a window or behind a grill or to someone aboard a boat dancing in the waters, which has a familiar and everyday quality as though in Venice it were the natural element of man. The conversation of the Venetians is not shouted, dramatic or gestured like that of the South, it is placid, graceful, civilized but no less witty and rich in humour. I think there are little examples of scintillating conversation, sparkling like that of two gondoliers engaged in a witty exchange, while they are serenely gliding past each other. The Venetians possess the humour of people who take life as it comes, who smooth out every situation, who have no need to rush about, who have plenty of time to exercise their minds in the best way. Venetian people have always seemed to me gifted by an intellectual level higher than that required by their often modest crafts, bound up with the economy of tourism, far and away the main source of income of the city. The Venetians seem to accept with tranquil philosophy and humour their destiny as descendants of a people who were amongst the richest and most prestigious in the world; the necessity of having to take advantage to survive, of the glory and the beautiful things from the past: like certain present day owners of English Country Houses who survive by opening them to the public who pay to see the Halls of their ancestors.

In Venice one can still breathe the grandeur of the past everywhere. Not only in the churches overflowing with works of art or in the palaces of the Grand Canal, but also in the people who inhabit it. There is around the Venetians a remote but living awareness of being the heirs of a glorious history and of excellence in every sphere. The Venetian gondolier is rather like the captain of a ship who had to turn necessity into virtue, who bent his will to destiny but who has never ceased to remember his past. Even if he is limited to gliding along the canal with his oar, we can not stop seeing in him the descendent of the daring seamen who used to sail in the thousand ships of which we can still see the shape in the paintings of Carpaccio, issuing forth from the Arsenal still vividly red at the far end of the shell-shaped city. And onto these is projected the shadow of the ancient merchants of both land and sea who feared nothing, and penetrated even into prohibited and unknown worlds like Marco Polo. Venice is a city which for centuries now has continued to come down from the incredible peak of richness and prestige which she had reached. But she has never forgotten that peak and she is still proud of it. It is the source of that aristocratic aura which still surrounds her and at the same time it underlies the philosophical principles of her people. To remind them that the things of man, even the most excellent, are dominated by the law of impermanence, and that all the historical flames, however great, are turned quickly into ashes and into memory.

Everything in Venice still speaks of greatness and decline, strongly intertwined with each other as though they were facets of a single reality. Venice is one of those places in the world which has become almost the symbol of the concept of decline. The end of the Republic in 1797, has sort of crystallized in time the extremely long decline of Venice, transforming it into a kind of unalter-

able category of the mind. All the great decadents, from Proust to Thomas Mann, from Hofmannsthal to Rilke, from Hesse to Visconti have dedicated to Venice great pages and great films, because Venice excites the feeling of the end of things, of their crumbling, of their ruin. Venice was also for them the place where one could come to surrender to death or to disappear, as happens in *Death in Venice* by Thomas Mann, or *Missing Venice* by Mario Bonfantini.
Even the moral decadence of the eighteenth-century, the delirium of senility of the decrepit Republic which Napoleon would have put out with a puff, have come to play a part in the myth of Venice and her extraordinary spells. They have become one of her facets, of the veils by which she is surrounded; one of the echoes which reverberate into her mysterious caverns.
Venice is like a woman with a hundred faces. She is the "Mediterranean Mother Goddess", the female archetype which emerges from the water in Fellini's *Casanova*. She is the bourgeois, curious and gossiping, of the comedies of her best playwright. She is the enigmatic aristocrat concealing her own face behind her Carnival veiled mask. She is the peasant who cries her wares in the market. She is the seasoned traveller to faraway lands. Also the courtesan richly endowed with jewels and eroticism, surrounded by an indefinable hint of the Orient. The East is also one of the resonances which one can gather in the magical Venetian shell. The domes of St. Mark's, especially if seen apart, above the surrounding buildings, have something of the mosque. In Venice there is the Warehouse of the Turks. In Venetian painting from Carpaccio to Gentile Bellini, there are details which recall the world of Turkey and the Middle East. I do not know how, but even the decadence and the sense of ending acquire in Venice something graceful, glittering, fairylike, theatrical. Within the lores and myths of Venice, there are no dichotomies or contrasts, but everything mingles with smiling grace, everything comes together as it does in her celebrated Carnival. In every fold of the reality and legends of Venice there still

shine the alluring ornaments of the ladies of the eighteenth century, with wigs, patches, painted eyes, sparkling jewels, rustling silk gowns, and satin slippers, which glitter in the theatre of Goldoni and in the Conversation Pieces of Pietro Longhi. In some way the image of Venice is still tied up with the eighteenth century. Although it is a city bustling with life, she evokes still, after more than two centuries, minuets and theatre foyers, decorated like jewel-boxes, Goldonian exchanges and the notes of Vivaldi. But if in the image of Venice the eighteenth century is prevailing, even in the shapes of the palaces mirrored in the Grand Canal, or in the style of the furniture lacquered in green and gold, all the periods and all the styles fuse together within the magic atmosphere of the city. At every step, at every turn of the oar or the propeller, one comes face to face with buildings of Gothic, fifteenth century, Renaissance, Baroque and nineteenth century styles. There is even the twentieth century of the Guggenheim Palace. Indeed the Palazzo Masieri designed by the great Frank Lloyd Wright — which gave rise to so much argument and then was never built — would not have seemed out of place. Venice fuses all the styles with incredible ease. She mixes the stylistic details of all the periods in her timeless dimension, in her existence as though outside history. Every age is represented here because nothing in it has been destroyed, and her exceptional qualities have in some way stopped the possible actions of vandals, whether from outside or within, and the fury of the renovators which has caused so much hideous damage in other cities. Where Venice is concerned everything stops. Rome and Florence experienced bombardments and artillery battles. Venice not. Her beauty succeeded in containing even the unleashed passions of men at war. Venice emanates from within herself something which has always saved her, which has preserved her from man's damage. It seems to involve also the fear of her ending but only by very slow means, beyond our concept of time, such as the change in the sea level which makes her sink a few millimetres every year, or the high tides due to the weather conditions and to the movements of the lagoon waters. Venice seems to have a unique and particular relationship with the sense of an end, in a certain way because she has already stepped out of time and entered into a fictitious dimension, theatrical, Carnivalesque, totally artistic and aesthetic.

Venice is also the place where to imagine men as actors, like Shakespearean ghosts who flit amongst the wings in a theatre. *Of actors, in Venice,* is the title of a novel by a Venetian writer, Carlo della Corte. Venice is in a certain way like a great theatre. St. Mark's Square with its great Procuratie and elegant arcades looks like a vast backdrop. One has the impression of finding oneself amidst the scenery representing an ideal city with diminishing perspective born in the mind of an Utopian architect of the Renaissance. But every angle of Venice seems like the background to a theatrical action, or simply to life, which is like an eternal theatre. Venice is a city, fictitious and theatrical even in her labyrinthine character and in her incredible capacity to falsify distances. What seems to be very remote at times you may reach in a few steps, and her maze of alleyways hides fantastic shortcuts. Sometimes the opposite happens.

In Venice life and theatre seem to live side by side, to be the same thing. Carlo Goldoni, to whom the whole of life seemed like a theatrical performance, could not have been anything but Venetian.

The Venetian theatricality is good-humoured, homely, conversational, full of graceful and affected gestures, even if in the background there is the faint suspicion that men are only shadows and ghosts. As Goldoni noted, in Venice everything is predisposed to be a place of theatre. It is enough to glance down a little canal, enter a little square, or into "The Coffee Shop", and one already sees the backdrop and the characters. Any pretext is enough to start the action: a comic scene, a gossip, a rumour, a fan.

The theatre is a diversion, a representation of fictitious reality, appearance, phenomena, and Venice is also all this. The grand cafés of St. Mark's Square, with their tables in the open, the drapes, the small orchestras, the ornate and painted panels of the interior are the most scenographic one can imagine. Perhaps the café was truly born in Venice to create a setting in which to mirror the intrinsic theatricality of life. The café has a Venetian soul. It is a place in which to gather news about one's neighbours. It is a place where one lives in the open and in which one can feel one is taking part in the comedy of life. Therefore Venice in her decline invented it and loved it, as much as she loved the theatre and the Carnival.

Carnival has been reborn and has had an immediate, overwhelming success, as happens to every Venetian initiative. As much as she is a theatrical city, Venice is therefore, also a Carnival city. Carnival is performance, fiction, masquerade, theatricality. It is a loud and colourful statement of the fact that man is an actor, a shadow that passes through the universe for an ephemeral and fleeting moment. Carnival is a way to bring to the surface and give shape and form to all the dramas that we carry within us, all the subconscious fears, the removed obsessions; a way to bring them out in a playful manner to make us believe we are not afraid of them, to wrap them up in overacting and load them with an exorcistic and liberating quality.

Carnival never lacks the symbols of death, old age, illness, war and slaughter. It means joy and liberation, amusement and simulation, a grotesque mixture of the many faces of life, a deformed image of it. Therefore Carnival has played, and still plays, such an important role in the life of Venice. For that reason we are attracted to it; because it is the plastic and colourful realization of all that we carry within us concerning joy and fear and pain. And because, as Italo Calvino says in his *Invisible Cities*, in every city there is a little bit of Venice.

Carlo Sgorlon

VENICE

"I saw from out the wave
her structure rise
As from the stroke
of the enchanter's wand..."

G. Byron

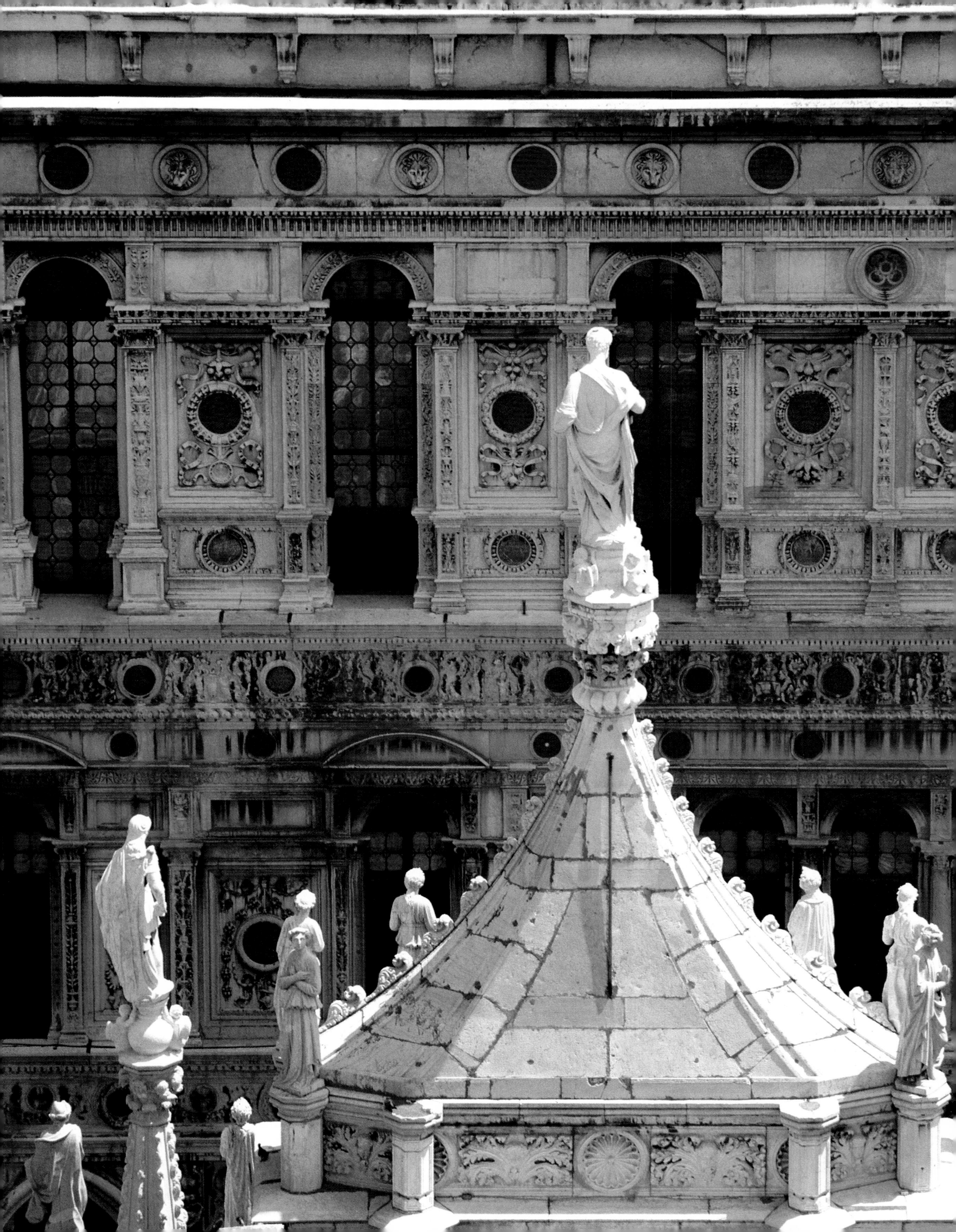

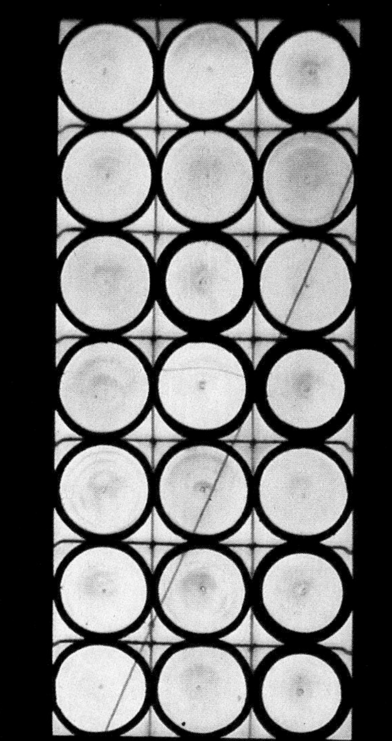
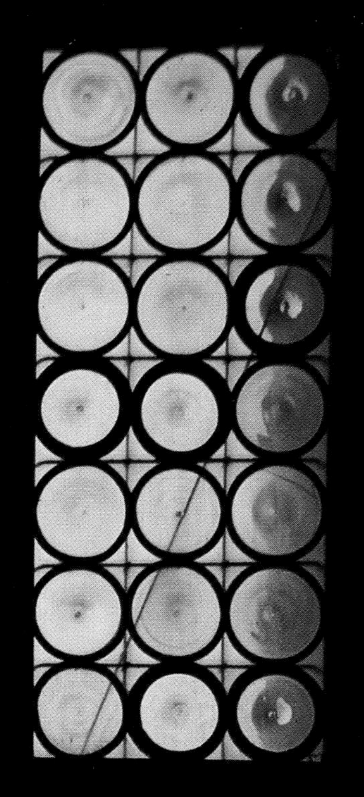
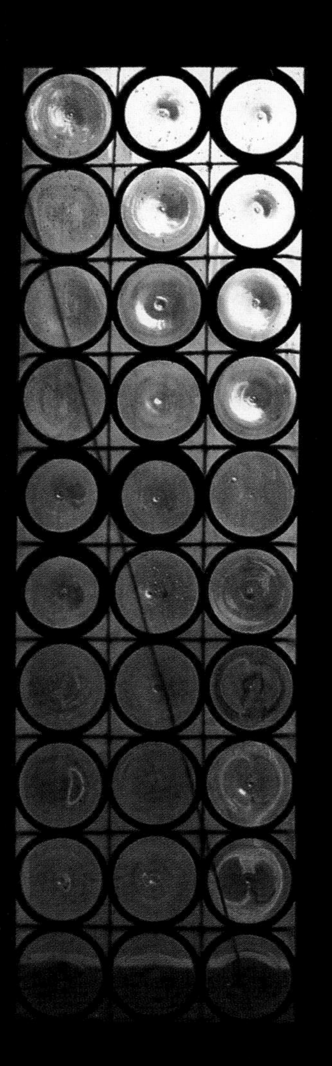

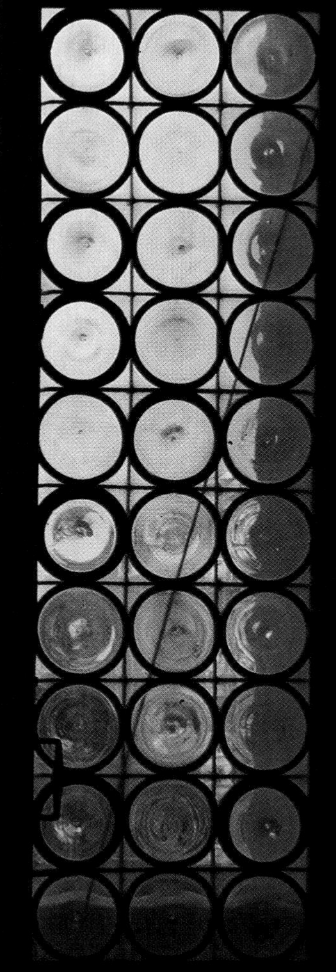

CINZANO

PAX EVAN
TIBI GELI
MAR STA
MEVS

SICACTVS
CHRISTI

TEA-ROOM

2

◁ 34

35

ACCADEMIA DI BELLE ARTI
1050
GALLERIE

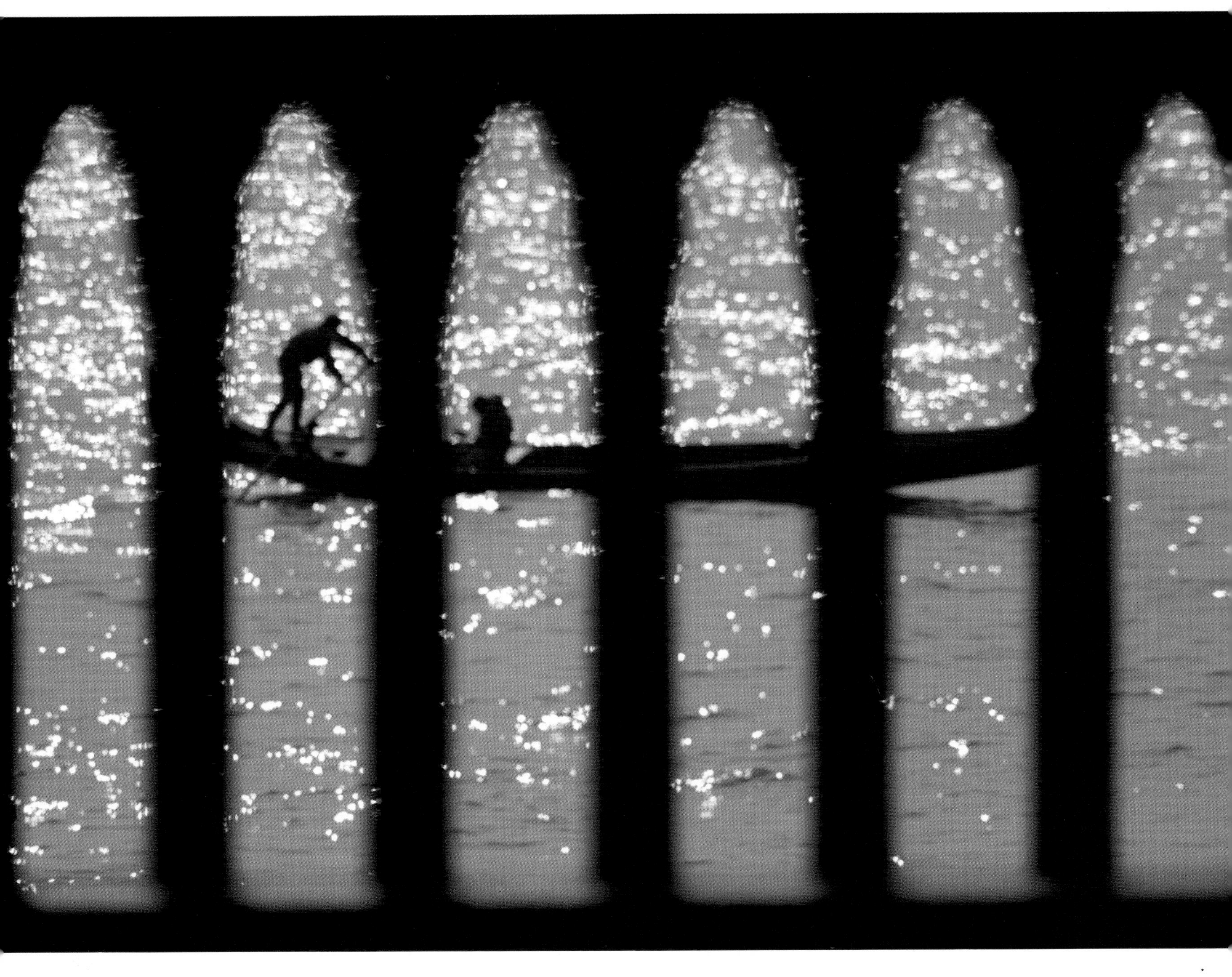

◁ 49

SOTOPORTEGO VA
IN CORTE BAROZZI

INTERNATIONAL FUND FOR MONUMENTS
RESTAURO DELLA SCALA
CONTARINI DEL BOVOLO

56

57

FORMOSA

59

61

62

72

PONTE DE LA
MALVASIA VECHIA

PONTE
STORTO

PONTE
STORTO

ALLE DEL DOSE
DA PONTE

93

94

Tiziano Rizzo

"The most noble and singular"

One wonders how this city, so noble and singular, could have flowered on this little stretch of land, in this lagoon once deserted and marshy, dotted with little barren islands, to become a city glowing with art, the radiating centre of such a high level of culture.
Beyond the legends, rhetorical celebrations and poetic inventions, it must be asserted that Venice was born from necessity, and through it, from the initial instinct of survival, developed her own history.
Forced by the barbarian invasions to abandon the towns and the villages of the mainland of the Veneto, and to take refuge along the shores and in the islands of the lagoon, (the first migrations date back to the descent of Alaric and the Visigoths in 408, and of Attila and the Huns in 452; the major and historically most certain flow took place with the invasion of the Langobards, between the second half of the sixth and the beginning of the seventh centuries), the first inhabitants of the future Venice had to change their way of life, turning themselves from farmers into fishermen and salt gatherers, exchanging horses for boats, the river water for rain water, and houses for pile-dwellings. If they wanted to survive — and they wanted to, daringly, they had to dedicate themselves absolutely to re-inventing life, with constantly finding ways and means to overcome nature rich only in fish, game, fruit and salt, but also and above all, that element which for a thousand years was to safeguard Venice from every attack: the shallow, inaccessible waters of the lagoon, a defence much more reliable than the walls of any other mediaeval city. It was this defence which provided the opportunity to establish the basis of a new social system and the foundations of an incomparable city, safe from every assault, and to change the original dependence on the Byzantine empire to absolute autonomy.
The limitation of means and the hostile environment called for an extraordinary zeal, adequate to the exceptional quality of the situation.
There arose what later Goethe would call a "Republic of beavers". Like these genial, persistent, mutually helpful rodents which dig their dens along the waterways sealing them with splinters and shavings, and costruct dams and bridges with branches, the first Venetians, finding themselves obliged to make a virtue of necessity, took to organizing the unstable territory of the lagoon, subject to tides and river sedimentations, to strengthening the banks of the winding canals among the clusters of islands, few of which had emerged, in ancient times, above the maximum level of the water, so to be inhabited — perhaps just a third of the present urban area. By means of operations — one can imagine to what extent — laborious and difficult, they undertook the work of draining and strengthening the islands which has not ceased up to to-day, and which would continue through time running parallel to the growth of power of the city. The date of the birth of Venice, strictly speaking, that of the

very historic centre, can be fixed in the period immediately following the attempt to conquer the lagoon by Pepin, King of Italy, son of Charlemaine, in the year 810. Driven by the wish to subject the surviving Byzantine duchy, he conquered Grado, Eraclea and Chioggia, but was stopped at Malamocco, on the Venetian shore, and had to retreat. After the danger was over, it was decided to transfer the capital of the duchy into the heart of the lagoon, into the safer Realtine islands, around which, between the ninth and the tenth centuries, little by little, the territorial and political unity of the rising state was being organized. At the same time navigation in the Mediterranean developed and grew together with trade with Byzantium and the East, of which Venice conquered the monopoly with armed forays against the Slavs and the Saracens. The year 1000, with the conquest of Dalmatia carried out by Doge Pietro Orseolo II and the act of submission and loyalty of the people of the Adriatic coast, from the gulf of Quarnaro to the Mouth of Cattaro, marks the conclusion of centuries of work organising the foundation, and the beginning of the establishment, of the Serenissima Repubblica.
Notwithstanding the harsh internal battles between families and factions for supremacy, the city was growing. More than on the advanced political system based on a particular form of democracy, the solidity of Venice relied mostly on loyalty, that feeling of absolute faithfulness to the fatherland which was rooted into and was nourished by the common troubled origins. The devotion and attachment to its own water-land, the prosperity offered by the dominion of the Adriatic assured in the XI century and by the extension of trade with the Levant, obtained with the acquisition of ports of call and markets in the XII century, gave the opportunity and obliged the Venetians to show concretely the acquired grandeur with the creation of the Dominant City. There were three vital nucleuses: St. Mark's with the Doge's Palace, the political, cultural and religious centres; the Arsenal, the military and shipbuilding centre; and the Rialto, the commercial and financial centre. Not by chance the urban planning of the three centres was established on dates very close together so as to make legendary those forty years between 1063 and 1104, during which are included the reconstruction of the basilica and the setting up of the markets of the Rialto and the foundation of the Arsenal. Neither is their positioning casual: in a dominant position looking out onto the vast basin into which sailed the ships coming from every corner of the known world, were the Palace and the Basilica of gold: while the Arsenal was hidden and guarded by high walls; and the market in the heart of the city, easily reachable through the wide, splendid way of the Grand Canal, whose sides began to be enriched by palaces always more sumptuous. All around, on the little islands arose houses, churches and shops.
The element which conditioned Venice from her very origins in every one of her urban traits was the water. Behind the obviousness of the assertion some aspects of the city are hidden, which often pass unobserved for those who go through *le calli, i campi, le corti, le salizade, le rughe,* the bridges, *i campielli, le fondamente, i rami, le rive, i rii terrà* (also in toponomy there is absolute singularity). The

water (the canal, better the *rio*, in Venetian) was originally the only means of communication, the boat the only means of going from one island to another. The houses arose therefore, along the banks facing the water with boats tied up near the entrance "like domestic animals". Also the churches were built away from the water because, as a document of 1180 said, referring to the first inhabitants of the lagoon, "when they wanted to go to church, they went by canal as *aliam viam non habebant*" as "they had no other way". The houses grew in number and size, side by side along the banks and then, towards the interior of the islands, leaving a gap between them, the *calle*, whose narrowness was of course due to the small amount of land available, but also to the little importance given to moving around on foot, then almost non existent. Between the houses there opened what was called, with an essentially rustic term, *la corte*, where animals were reared and kitchen gardens cultivated. The largest space on the island, which generally extended behind the church, was (and is) *il campo*, thus also a toponym of farming origin, truly a field with trees where cattle grazed. In the cities of the mainland, which one may call "normal", the big palaces face on to the squares: in the abnormal city, the palaces, the houses, the churches have their main facade turned towards the canal, not towards the *campi*, which constitute the Venetian squares. The rule — if we can talk about a rule — was in force until the XV century, that of the maximum splendour of the Serenissima, which was preceded by two hundred devastating years of incessant wars for the supremacy of the sea, necessary for the expansion of trade. The cause of those two hundred years of conflict was the fourth Crusade in 1204, the first in which Venice was directly engaged.
The unscrupulous shrewdness, the pragmatism of the Venetians in the operations which prepared the Crusade, remained exemplary, whilst legendary remained the figure of the ninety-year-old, blind Doge Enrico Dandolo who lead it. Here is a brief résumé of the events. The French nobles who had decided to become crusaders, sent Geoffrei de Villehardouin to Venice, to negotiate the transport to the Holy Land of 35,000 men ad 4,500 horses, whom they foresaw gathering. In exchange for the means of transport and for a year's supply of food, the old Doge asked for 85,000 silver marks (around double the annual income of the king of France). Furthermore in exchange for 50 fully armed galleys with 6,000 crew, he asked for the overall bounty and all the lands that might be conquered. In his report Villehardouin wrote that "the fully equipped fleet was of so much beauty and excellence, that no Christian ever saw one more beautiful or more excellent". At the reckoning, the Crusaders realized they could no longer fulfil this very onerous contract. The Venetians, on the contrary, who perhaps from the beginning had foreseen it and had intentionally kept their demands very high, offered the Crusaders the opportunity to settle the debt: the reconquest of the rebellious Zara. After re-obtaining the Dalmatian city, Enrico Dandolo imposed a second detour from the original route, and the fleet, instead of heading towards Jerusalem where the Crusader army was begging for help, turned towards Constantinople. The capital of the Empire capitulated in April 1204, after almost

a year of siege, and Venice obtained together with new important dominions what she wanted most; which was, to put on the Byzantine throne an Emperor friend, Alessio il Giovane, overturning the hateful dynasty of the Comneni. Whatever the successive developments of the Crusade, here the astute and crafty Venice came out of it triumphant; but her expansion which seemed now impossible to stop, caused the outbreak of the big conflict with Genoa which took place first in the East, and then from the Aegean to the Adriatic with the heavy defeat of Venice at Curzola, 1298, and which was protracted until the war of Chioggia, 1378-1381, with the decisive victory of the Serenissima.

Although engaged in such very expensive events, undermined by internal plots (famous was that lead by Bajamonte Tiepolo in 1310) and by uprisings and rebellions in the overseas dominions, especially in Crete; repeatedly overturned by earthquakes, floods and frightening fires, Venice went on with the intense work of the reorganization of its social structure, culminating in the concentration of power in the hands of the aristocracy the (*Serrata del Maggior Consiglio*, which limited the number of members of the Great Council, the Supreme organ of Government, of 1268) and of the construction and reconstruction of buildings always more sumptuous: churches, palaces, monasteries, hospices and houses. Visitors, coming from their severe and gloomy towns on the mainland, found themselves spellbound. They were princes and kings, scholars, ambassadors, great merchants, common people attracted by the fame of the enchanting city, but above all, by the Venetian organisation of journeys to the Holy Land. The Crusaders who under the pretext of the liberation of the Holy Sepulchre tended to slow down Muslim expansionism, had fostered the myth of Jerusalem. Venice, the natural bridge to the Orient, profited from the favourable opportunity to diffuse her own image of a golden city, lovable, happy and pious, and to put to advantage the innate commercial talent of her inhabitants and of her government. She invented the holy journeys, very expensive and very exhausting, which lasted six months from the moment of departure to the moment of return, for those who had survived disease, privations and the attacks of pirates. Journeys extremely difficult which people of every condition underwent: ecclesiastics and nobles like the Count of Derby, to whom the far-sighted Republic gave special treatment, furnishing him with a personal galley and paying all his expenses. This favour was repaid a hundredfold when the Count, who became Henry IV of England, showed he had not forgotten the journey completed (incognito) in 1392. Among other things Venice offered to the pilgrims waiting there for departure, an authentic "collection" of sacred relics formed around that very precious one of the remains of St. Mark appropriated in Alexandria in Egypt far back in 828. Even from this singular attraction which, with irreverent realism was defined as the industry of relics — just like the holy journeys were identified as the most ancient tourist industry — the Venetians took unimaginable advantage for the development of crafts and for the increase in business for inn-keepers and merchants.

They were consolidating the solid social fabric of the city-state,

sustained by the patrician families who reserved for themselves the task of governing, allotting, alternating and mutually controlling in the numerous offices in which the administration of power was articulated. The carpenters, the goldsmiths, the glass makers, the stone masons, the weavers, the tailors, the coopers, the minor and major merchants, were joined into corporations, the *Scuole* (Guilds) which had, as their institutional aims, pious practices, the defence of common interests, mutual assistance and charitable works. Every member was obliged to pay annual taxes to the Corporation, and every Corporation had to give to the State a large amount, a kind of indirect tax which increased in times of war, when the Guilds also had to provide armed men for the State according to their size. Through such a subtle policy the power of the State could indirectly intervene, appearing only in the background and only as the guarantee of the security of the destiny of the country, generating, on the other hand, strong competition between the Guilds, for its own advantage. The cunning system wrapped the city up in a tight network, through whose threads every imposition and every control was possible, which the ancestral loyalty made acceptable. With an utterly different attitude the numerous colonies of foreigners (Germans, Persians, Greeks, Albanians and people from Lucca etc.) were obliged to accept the repeated invitations to fill the coffers of the State with "gifts", a sort of residence tax, particularly heavy for the Jewish community who, however, in spite of segregations and vexations, found in Venice a less tough climate that in any other European city.
The XV century gave substance to the Venetian policy — the so-called "of the mainland", which marked the beginning of the decline of the maritime Republic. It was not, at least at the beginning, a mere thirst for conquest; the systematic penetration into the mainland which took the dominion of the Serenissima as far as the river Mincio, had necessity as its principal characteristic. The total ruin risked in the war of Chioggia, had shown that it was indispensable to ensure a better control of the territories on the mainland; the Turks infiltrated in every part of the colonial empire, imposing the urgency of new energy, above all of men, which only the mainland could supply. The progressive, constant expansion which lasted the whole of the XV century with the annexation of Padua and Verona (1404-1405), of Aquileia (1418-1420), Brescia, Bergamo and Crema, then of the Polesine (1484), and part of Puglia and Romagna (1504), created around the Republic a climate, always more resentful, but not without reason, of diffidence and intrigue, which became substantial in the League of Cambrai, an alliance of almost all the European powers — Austria, France, Spain, the Papal State — against Venice. The battle of Agnadello, on the 14th May, 1509, with the French victory, marked the end of Venetian expansion.
Notwithstanding the exhausting draining of men and means imposed by the continuous conflicts, the city reached between the XV and the XVI centuries her greatest splendour, assuming the aspect which despite the considerable operations which took place in the succeeding centuries, especially in the XIX century, is still today substantially present. Most of the ancient Venetian-Byzantine civil

and religious buildings, were radically modified, enlarged or substituted by edifices made more graceful by the flowery Gothic style which in Venice shone with her own particular splendour — and then with the great architecture of the Renaissance, mainly developed with the contribution of the Lombard masters (the Solari, the Cordussi) and the Tuscans (the Sansovino). Regarding which one can observe, that for a strange, and one could say capricious, phenomenon, whilst Venetian painting was born almost through spontaneous germination and flowered and prospered as though fed by an intrinsic vigour, drawing little from other sources, diffusing instead important lessons everywhere (it is enough to mention the names of the Vivarini, of the Bellini, of Carpaccio, of Giorgione, of Cima, of Titian, of Paolo Veronese, Tintoretto, the Tiepolo and Guardi...) architecture and sculpture were from early times principally imported arts. This particular "phenomenon" drew its origin perhaps from the natural surroundings of the Venetian lagoon and from her mainland itself, where colour and light prevail over plasticity of form. The truth is that in Venice the balanced simplicity of lines, surfaces and mass, codified by Renaissance architecture, was combined with a native, unavoidable pictorial feeling which in the XVII century found its greatest interpreter in Baldassarre Longhena, a Venetian.
The incessant re-kindling of wars in the XVII and XVIII centuries — perennial contendents were the Turks and later the Austrians — and the consequent progressive reduction of Mediterranean dominions, culminated in 1718 with the handing over of the last territories, marking the end of Venetian power; but those were not the only causes. Two far-off events had undermined her trade, fundamental source of wealth and strength: the discovery of America in 1492 which opened important and new prospects for Europe and — more immediately — the sea route towards India opened by Vasco de Gama (1498), with the valuble help of the map of the world by the Venetian Fra' Mauro. The Portuguese explorer, on his return to Lisbon, recounted how in Calcutta one could buy one hundred kilos of spices for two or three ducats, while in Venice one paid seventy for them. Meanwhile, England and Holland had entered the Mediterranean markets, and in Florence the production of wool and silk were progressing... A vice was closing with a relentless march and progressive damage, around Venice who did not know, or did not want, or rather could not, turn her own interests outside the Mediterranean. Exhausted, unprepared to face the ocean with proper ships, with her old vigour weakened by a soft and luxurious life, the proud city retreated more and more into herself, preparing herself to open her gates and her treasures to Napoleon's army.
On the 12th May, 1797, the Great Council, presided over by Doge Ludovico Manin "the faint-hearted", as the people called him, held its last meeting and abdicated. Three days later the French troops entered the city after a long siege. On the following 17th October, with the treaty of Campoformio, Napoleon ceded Venice to Austria (thus crowning an old dream), using her as if she were his own. He had promised the ambassadors of the Serenissima that "he would be an Attila for Venice". And he was. He began the barbaric work of

devastation, and stripped from the churches and the palaces hundreds of works of art, entire valuable libraries, transporting to Paris the golden horses from the Loggia of Saint Mark's (which would later return to Venice). He went on and increased it during the second domination (1806-1814) which followed the first Austrian period. To understand to what extent and with what outcome the Napoleonic storm passed, on whose trail was unleashed — though with effects not so nefarious — the wave of the Hapsburgs, the following alone is sufficient. Of the 187 churches existing in Venice (including the major islands, Murano, Burano and Torcello) at the fall of the Republic, after the Napoleonic decrees and the Austrian domination, only 101 were counted. Out of the 86 churches no longer existing, 70 were demolished and the remaining sixteen survived being used for different purposes — warehouses, industrial workshops, schools, meeting halls. At the same time an endless draining of works of art took place, unimaginable for those who have not read those two valuable volumes which make up *Venezià scomparsa* (The Lost Venice), by Alvise Zorzi and the wide documentation which accompanies them.

1797 sealed not only the end of a State but constituted also the premise of radical changes in the urban structure of the city with the serious risk of definitive overturning. The dawn of the industrial era opened revolutionary perspectives all over the world. But Venice, because of her very particular structure, more than any other city, was put into danger by innovatory ferments. If in other places those ferments could find relief and be realized in the destruction of the surrounding walls of the cities, to "modernise" and to "make bourgeois", in Venice they could not express themselves except within that which for a millennium had been her firmest defence, the water.

The wholesale destruction, the covering of the little canals, the draining of large parts of the lagoon succeeded one after the other without ceasing. Three churches with the adjacents convents — we cite some examples — were torn down to make way for large public gardens: where the last two tracts of the Procuratie stood, which, with the church of San Geminiano by Sansovino, closed the Piazza opposite the Basilica, the Napoleonic wing was constructed with the State Entrance to the Royal Palace (the Procuratie Nuove), lived in by Eugene Beauharnais, the adopted son of Napoleon, who ordered, furthermore, the demolition of a great building which hid the view from his apartments towards the basin, and the layout of those gardens which are still called the Royal Gardens.

Later in 1846, the construction of the railway bridge across the lagoon, marked the break of the thousand years of proud isolation of Venice. The building of the "terminal", of the warehouses, of offices, involved the demolition of four big palaces, one church, shops and houses. Movement on foot , already taking over from that on the water, had to be made easier going towards the centre of the city, requiring the sacrifice, already unavoidable, but often imposed with unscrupulous ease, of other palaces, of other ancient habitations, other religious buildings: the great straight route from the Railway Station to San Bartolomeo (near the Rialto bridge) was completed with the opening of the Strada Nova in 1871, five years after the annexing of Venice to the Kingdom of Italy. Other destruction and demolition, besides those already mentioned before, followed the first opening, made by the railway bridge, stretching throughout the XIX and part of the XX centuries. In this century the operations of major importance were turned to modest buildings, whose development called for the draining of vast marginal areas of the city, and even the creation of new islands such as Sant'Elena and Sacca Fisola. Also the bridge, finished in 1933, caused inevitable alterations in the urban texture. Actually, the life of the city takes place to-day principally in the Venice of the XIX and the XX centuries.

1.2.3

Generated — it seems — by the combined phenomena of the sinking of the land and the rising of the water level, the Lagoon *par excellence* was always the enemy-friend of Venice. The low sea-level, the intricate network of the winding navigable canals which are deeper, constituted an insurmountable defence which lasted for a thousand years against every enemy attack.
The threats had always come from the precariousness natural in that environment, menaced by those rivers which, flowing into the lagoon, altered with massive sedimentation the uncertain balance, and whose estuaries, therefore, had to be directed to the open sea, over and over again from the XIII to the XVII centuries. The sea, another powerful and constant threat, changed the face of the lagoon swallowing tens of little islands once inhabited and rich in churches and convents: of the sixty which dotted the lagoon around the city there remain to-day not even thirty (in picture No 1 the island of San Lazzaro degli Armeni).

4

Thomas Mann said that to reach Venice from the mainland across the bridge is like entering through the servants' door. The true main gate is the huge basin which stretches in front of St. Mark's: from the intense green of the gardens as far as the white Punta della Dogana at the mouth of the Grand Canal. Here the city used to show her solemn and enchanted face to Kings, to Popes, to the ambassadors of the European powers, to great merchants who approached her from the sea: it was the face of the Powerful One.
A large number of ships of every type and size lay at anchor or ploughed the waters: others penetrated through the canals into the city of which one could guess the fervid activity (see also No 21).

5

One day in an unknown year in the second half of the XII century, a small fleet returning fron Constantinople unloaded — amongst other things — on the bank near Saint Mark's, two huge granite columns, one ash grey and the other reddish. A third one, according

to an old chronicle *"descargandola cazete ne l'acque e mai non se ne pote averla* (on unloading, fell into the water and could never be recovered)".
The city-state grew in power and took particular care to embellish herself with sumptuous works. From every voyage along the shores of the Adriatic, from Egypt and from Greece, the Venetian navigators returned laden with inscriptions, statues, precious marbles, low-reliefs and capitals. We have no means of knowing whether they were acquired by honest purchase, by transaction, by looting rather than really and truly by theft, and it is preferable that this matter is covered by the mist of time. The "recoveries" — we shall call them — of major size, were the two monoliths which rise in Piazzetta San Marco, towards the water's edge, erected there in 1172 by that Nicolò — builder and architect from Bologna — to whom, since he had succeeded in the task, was granted permission to gamble between the two columns and was therefore nicknamed Barattieri (gambler).
On the grey column, the one nearest the Doge's Palace, is placed a bronze winged lion of uncertain origin (Etruscan Art, according to some, Persian or even Chinese, according to others), repeatedly restored; on the red column, next to the Library, stands the marble statue of San Teodoro, the first patron of the city, popularly called *Todaro*.
Between the two columns, between the sea and the sky, capital sentences were carried out from the earliest times, perhaps not very many if compared to other States, but still awe-inspiring because of the public proclamations throughout the city which ensured that they were an example to all.

6

The basin of San Marco is enclosed by the island of San Giorgio Maggiore, facing the Doge's Palace, once called the Island of the Cypresses, donated in the year 982 by Doge Tribuno Memmo to the Benedictines who founded a monastery there. Five centuries afterwards there arose the noble buildings which give it its profile. The church, a work of art by Andrea Palladio, erected between 1566 and 1610, rich in paintings by Tintoretto, by Jacopo Bassano, by Sebastiano Ricci and by Carpaccio. The elegant *campanile* which was reconstructed in its upper part at the end of the XVIII century with the angel which rotates by the action of the wind; the monastery, whose older facade stretches for nearly one hundred and thirty metres along the Western bank of the island, towards the Canal of the Giudecca.

7

In 1589 the Senate of the Republic decided on the building of a new prison beyond the little canal which laps against the Doge's Palace, the seat of Government and justice, giving the commission to the young architect, Antonio Contino, nephew of the builder of the

Rialto bridge, for an elegant bridge, convenient and "with maximum security" — as we would say to-day — connecting the two buildings. People say that in designing it (completed in 1600) Contino drew inspiration from the outline of the gondola. Through its double covered passage — one for coming, one for going — the prisoners were taken to the presence of the Magistrates: the popular imagination saw them moving along in chains to the sumptuous rooms of the *Avogadori,* sighing in sorrow and anxiety for the fate which awaited them, and from that was born the romantic name of The Bridge of Sighs. Attracted by the fame of the bridge, many overlook the marble group which embellishes the corner of the Doge's Palace near the Ponte della Paglia (The Bridge of Straw). The beautiful work, executed between the end of the XIV and the beginning of the XV centuries, probably by Lombard sculptors, represents the drunken Noah, unsteady on his legs, overhung by a vine, from which plant, according to Biblical tradition, he for the first time made wine.

8.9.10

The season which many Venetians prefer is the late autumn, when the clamour of mass tourism, superficial and unaware, dies down, and the city regains the silence and her own voice which the mist wraps round with the melancholy of her now closed destiny.

11.12.13.14.15.16.17

The Palazzo Pubblico, the Palazzo Civile, the dwelling of the Doges and seat of the highest Offices of the Government, was always the concrete symbol of the unity of the Republic, the expression of her strength and her opulence.
Following the fires and the changing needs of the city, the Palace was reconstructed in the course of the centuries until around the middle of the XV century it acquired the definitive aspect it still has to-day. There was a passage from the original truly Byzantine style to the Renaissance Gothic, an admirable example of elegant beauty and vigour in which architecture, sculpture and colour contribute to the perfect balance of the unity of the composition.
The State entrance to the Palazzo is the Porta della Carta (No 13 — whose name comes perhaps from the proximity of the *carte,* the papers, the State Archives, or from the scribes who near here wrote out documents and petitions). A masterpiece designed and carried out, or better one should say, chiselled, by Giovanni and Bartolomeo Bon, father and son, commissioned in 1448 by the Doge Francesco Foscari, who appears there, above the doorway kneeling before St. Mark's lion. Next to the superb gateway, set into the corner of the building which houses the Treasure of St. Mark's, is the celebrated group in porfiry known as the *Tetrarchi,* (No 14). But the four severe characters, armed with swords, joined in an embrace, are nothing to do with the Governors who ruled the Roman empire together with Diocletian. It is an Egyptian work from the IV century A.D., brought

to Venice by one of those galleys which ploughed the Mediterranean engaged at the same time in battle and trade.

18.19.20

"She is spacious and large and beautiful... and as Petrarch said, has no equal in all the world". In this way Francesco Sansovino, son of that Jacopo who was the protagonist of Venetian architecture of the XVI century, in his *Venezia, città nobilissima e singolare* (Venice, the most noble and singular city), introduced the chapter dedicated to the square, which was her political and cultural centre where the history of the city and of her architecture are summarised.
Until the middle of the XII century the area of the piazza was about half that of the present one, limited by a canal, called Batario, which ran parallel to the church of St. Mark's. During the reign of Sebastiano Ziani (1172-1178), that little canal was covered over and the first *Procuratie* were erected — so-called because they were the Seat of the Procurators, magistrates second only in importance to the Doge — re-built between the end of the XV and the beginning of the XVI centuries (No 19). At the bottom of the square there rose another church, dedicated to San Giminiano; next to the Campanile there were shops, the ancient hospice founded by Pietro Orseolo, and other buildings which were demolished in 1584 to make way for the Procuratie Nuove, designed by Vincenzo Scamozzi and finished by Baldassarre Longhena in 1640, taking as his model the Sansovinian Library which looks over the Piazzetta and of which the Procuratie Nuove are the extension.
A few years after the fall of the city to the French, the exquisite church of San Giminiano (reconstructed in the XVI century by Sansovino), the last stretch of the Procuratie Vecchie and part of the Nuove were pulled down and in their place was erected, designed by Giuseppe Soli, the Ala Nuovissima, better known as the Ala Napoleonica (Napoleonic Wing), because it was wanted by Bonaparte as the State Entrance to the Royal Apartments set up in the Procuratie Nuove.
A characteristic element of the square is the decorative design of the paving stones, whose elegance one can fully appreciate if seen from above.

21

View of the city from the island of San Giorgio.

22.23.24

An ancient legend says that the Evangelist Mark during a stay on an island in the lagoon, was visited by an angel, who, with the words "*Pax tibi, Marce, evangelista meus*, Peace be unto you, Mark my evangelist", predicted that his mortal remains would find rest here. The prophesy was realised with the help of two Venetian travellers, Buono da Malamocco and Rustico da Torcello who, according to

tradition, in the first year of the IX century, purloined the body of the Saint in Alexandria in Egypt and carried it home welcomed by celebrating crowds.
To house the very precious relics there arose next to the Ducal Castle the first church of St. Mark, consecrated in 832. Partially destroyed by a fire in 976, it was reconstructed by Pietro Orseolo the Doge who died in an aura of sanctity, who had to wait however until 1731 to be canonized. The expansion of territory and trade, source of an always greater income, induced the Venetians to rebuild the church, enlarging and enriching it, taking as their models the Great Temples of the East and in particular the church of the Twelve Apostles in Costantinople. The third church of Saint Mark, the "Doge's Chapel" which became the patriarchal seat only in 1807, had been consecrated in 1094. But only in the first half of the XIII century did there arise, on the same architectural scheme as the preceding building, the new facade, rich in marble, columns and mosaics, and at the end of the XIV, the final Gothic touch of arches and pinnacles was added, crowned by the fantastic cornice of statues and curling leaves (No 22). The statue of the Evangelist at the highest point of the arch and the four angels with golden wings are the work of Nicolò Lamberti, a Florentine sculptor working in Venice at the beginning of the XV century; the lion of Saint Mark was remade by Gaetano Ferrari in 1826 on the old model.
The splendid mosaics (Nos 23 and 24) which decorate the interior of the church are the product of the Venetian School formed about the year 1000 on the example of the Ravenna style first and then the Byzantine style, and developed between the XII and XIII centuries. From this period remain numerous and excellent examples in the great complex of the Domes, in the series of Biblical scenes, of the life of Christ and of St. Mark. Throughout the centuries the Basilica was gradually enriched with new mosaics in every corner, some of which were composed from the cartoons designed by the great masters Paolo Uccello, Tiziano Vecellio, Veronese, Pordenone...

25

The four gilded bronze horses which from the top of the loggia of the Basilica dominate the Piazza, are not those which the Doge Enrico Dandolo sent from Constantinople in 1204. The present ones are copies, placed there only recently, of the authentic four-horse chariot, taken away to shelter them from the nefarious agents which poison the air and eat into the bronze.
Their birth and their first vicissitudes are wrapped up in mystery and legend. For a long time they were believed to be Greek art of the IV-III centuries B.C.; more recently they were thought to be Roman, cast perhaps to decorate a triumphal arch. During the fourth Crusade the Doge Dandolo found them situated on the towers of the hippodrome of the capital of the Byzantine Empire where perhaps they had arrived from Rome in the IV century. The journey by sea from Costantinople to Venice was followed, six centuries later, by that from Venice to Paris in the last days of 1797. Napoleon wanted

them to decorate the entrance to the Palace of the Tuileries, then the Arch of Triumph of Carrousel. In 1815, on 13th December, the four horses returned to Venice and were put back on to the Loggia, to be taken down again twice during the two Great Wars. Finally, their sad, contested but definitive removal.

26.27

Gianfranco Morosini, ambassador to Constantinople, in a report of 1585 to the Venetian Senate, recounted how the Turks used to drink "a black water as hot as they can bear, which you make out of a seed which they call *kahvè* , which they say has the virtue of keeping a man awake". It is the first mention of coffee by an Italian. And the first to introduce coffee into Europe could not have been other than the Venetian a few years after the hint given by Morosini.
Although first considered as a medicine, people soon began to like it as a drink, and its use spread so rapidly that it induced people to open shops to drink the aromatic infusion. The first coffee shop was opened in 1683, naturally in St. Mark's Square, the *drawing room* of the city, under the Procuratie Nuove. Very soon others could be seen in every quarter and in the XVIII century almost all the shops around the Square were coffee-shops, distinguishable one from the other by their most fancy shop signs.
The one that remained the most celebrated, Florian's (No 27), was opened on 29th December 1720 by Floriano Francesconi, and consisted of two modest rooms which showed off the pretentious sign of "Venice Triumphant", a vain auspice in those years of the extreme decline of the Republic. Valentino Francesconi who took over twenty years after his uncle's death, changed the sign calling the shop "Florian" after its founder, a name which would become "the shop known all over the world", a meeting place for scholars, lords and beautiful ladies, conspirators and artists.
In 1858 the management passed into other hands and the famous coffee shop was completely renovated and enlarged, assuming the aspect that it still preserves, with the "Saletta of the Senate" with panels decorated by the painter Casa, representing "Progress" and "The Sciences", the Greek and Persian Rooms, the side rooms with portraits of illustrious men painted by Carlini, and the Gallery of the Seasons.
The Viennese Karl Hernold wrote: "Europe is the most beautiful part of the World; Italy is the most beautiful part of Europe; Venice is the most beautiful city in Italy; St. Mark's Square is the most beautiful square in Venice; Florian's is the most beautiful meeting place in the Piazza, therefore I drink my moka in the most beautiful place in the world".

28.29

Wearing that bizarre cap of Persian origin on one's head, called the *corno ducale* (the ducal horn), was always the maximum ambition of every member of the most noble Venetian families. Yet, at least in

the last centuries of the Republic, the power of the Doge was extremely limited as he had become a mere symbol of the city, surrounded by the pomp and glory, a figure almost inert, a prisoner in the Palace.
At the court of Louis XIV "to count like the Doge at Venice" meant one did not count at all. Nevertheless, to reach the ducal throne was always thought to be for a Venetian patrician and his family a great victory and a very high honour. Among others who succeeded, were Francesco Foscari, Doge from 1423 to 1457, vigorously portrayed by Lazzaro Bastianin — the painting kept in the Museo Correr (No 28) — and Antonio Venier, Doge from 1382 to 1400, represented kneeling, in the little marble statue (No 29), the masterpiece of Jacobello dalle Masegne, also kept in the Museo Correr.

30.31

"For tonight I have ordered the famous song of the gondoliers, who sing Tasso and Ariosto to a tune of their own invention. One must order it specially, because it is no longer a common thing, yet it is part of the legends of past times, almost forgotten. In the moonlight I got into a gondola with one singer on the prow and another on the stern; they started their song and sang alternately verse after verse... and the song spread across the silent waters" (Wolfgang Goethe, *Travels in Italy*).

32.33.34

The courtyard of the Doge's Palace, the island of San Giorgio in the snow, and a view of the city from the Campanile of St. Mark's.

35

Giustina Renier-Michiel, a Venetian noblewoman who held a renowned literary salon towards the end of the XVIII century, wrote: "The gondoliers are generally full of wit, finesse and insight; they are deft and gay, the vivacity of their replies and their words are pleasing and enchanting. They enjoy in particular the fame of having hearts frank, loyal and open, of being discreet, faithful, and most affectionate towards their masters". Contrary to her admiration is the opposite view of a scholar (not Venetian) of the XVI century, Tommaso Garzoni, who very differently sketches the natural character of the gondoliers: "All of them deport themselves during the day according to what they are, they have in their mouths vain oaths of all kinds, bringing down curses on people's heads that they may be visited by plague and disease, they may be hanged, put in the stocks, and whipped. In them one finds no sincerity, one discovers no manners and one sees no goodness".
Leaving aside the enthusiasm and the denigration, this Venetian figure, as ancient as the city of whose landscape he is an integral and necessary part, is defined in his most marked characteristic — a genuine pride of caste — in the praise of an old gondolier in the

Putta onorata (The Virtuous Maid) by Goldoni, about his own trade, thus talking to his young grandson "...and to do the trade of your father, your grandfather, your great-grandfather and all our family. We boatmen make up a body of people that one does not find in any other country in the world".

36

The Bridge of Straw, so called because here, in old times, they used to moor boats laden with straw for horses, for cows, for donkeys and also for mattresses, was one of the first to be built in stone, with the characteristic balustrades and little columns with small Gothic arches ornamented by carved pine cones each one different from the other. After the enlarging of the Riva degli Schiavoni carried out in 1782, the bridge was re-built doubled in size but respecting the original design.
As a result of its privileged position, the bridge has seen life in its many shades: along here used to pass many solemn processions; here were exposed the drowned bodies for recognition; from here people used to go to the famous inns of the Snake, of the Star, and of the Crown; here they used to hang the bodies of those condemned to be quartered.

37

View of the basin from the lower portico of the Doge's Palace. In the background the quay of the gondolas and the island of San Giorgio.

38

Two powerful Atlases support a shiny golden sphere, allegory of the world, on top of which Fortune is poised to pivot when the wind catches her sail. The group, placed on the Tower of the Customs House, dominated that exceptional corner of the basin of St. Mark where the Grand Canal and the Canale della Giudecca join together. In the background the dome of the church of the Salute, the synthesis and masterpiece of the pictorial sense of architecture of Baldassarre Longhena, a treasure-house of famous paintings of Titian, of Tintoretto, of Padovanino, of Palma the Younger, of Andrea Vicentino. This admirable church was built after the plague of 1630 and dedicated to the Madonna in token of gratitude for the end of the terrible pestilence.

39.40.41

The Gallery of the Accademia was born with the intention of housing there as much as it was possible to keep in Venice, of the immense patrimony of works of art resulting from the suppression and destruction of churches, convents and palaces in the Napoleonic era (1806-1814). Although only a minimal part of the great treasures could be saved from being deported to cities all over Europe to enrich their museums and collections, in the rooms of the Gallery the first important nucleus was formed — which little by little increased — of a collection which summarises the history of the whole of Venetian painting, from the Primitives to the Vivarini, from Cima to the Bellini, from Veronese to Tintoretto, to Tiepolo, from the Tempest of Giorgione, to the presentation of Mary in the Temple by Titian (No 40), to the Miracle of the Reliquar of the Cross by Carpaccio (No 39).

42.43

Views of the Grand Canal from the Rialto Bridge and the Accademia. What to-day appears nothing but a large water-way, sumptuous, enchanting, picturesque, but now limited in its use (the *Vaporetto*, a few boats, gondolas for tourists), was the true backbone of Venice. Topographically it is also thus: a big S which separates the city into two parts and it is at the same time its main artery into which all the little canals flow. But until the beginning of the last century, it was the very busy extension of the port, the way along which the ships from the lagoon reached the heart of the city, the Rialto, the commercial and financial centre.
The palaces which flank the Grand Canal in the course of its 3,750 metres bear witness to the development of Venetian architecture; some from the XIII and XIV century Byzantine period (Ca' Farsetti and Ca' Loredan, now the Town Hall, Ca' Da Mosto near the Rialto, the Fontego de' Turchi, rebuilt a hundred years ago according to the original model), numerous examples of the XV century Venetian Gothic (like the Ca' d'Oro, Ca' Foscari, Ca' Dario, the Gritti Palace Hotel, the Palazzo Contarini-Fasan, known as the house of Desdemona). The superb Vendramin-Calergi Palace was finished in the first years of the XVI century. In the following centuries many old buildings — because of their decrepit state as a result of fires, or from a wish for renewal — were pulled down and in their place arose the huge XVI century palaces (Ca' Corner, now the Prefettura, the Grimani Palace, now the Court of Appeal, the Manin Palace, now the Bank of Italy) beside others of more modest proportion, but no less noble, such as the elegant Palace of the Camerlenghi at the beginning of the Rialto bridge (No 42). Then in the XVII and XVIII centuries other monumental buildings (Ca' Pesaro, the Grassi Palace, Ca' Rezzonico) or, with classical echoes (Palazzo Moro-Lin "of the thirteen windows", the incomplete Ca' Venier dei Leoni, acquired by Peggy Guggenheim). Modest but easily distinguishable signs of the XIX century are left along the banks of the Grand Canal. Our century has limited itself (fortunately?) to the imitation of the Gothic (Casa Rava' at San Silvestro, the Pescheria of the Rialto), to the reconstruction of the Railway station and other minor operations and to the building of the most elegant bridge of the Scalzi designed by Eugenio Miozzi in 1934.

44

Near the bridge of the Greeks, on the canal of San Lorenzo, rises the beautiful XV century facade of palazzo Zorzi (see also No 46).

45

The Rialto Bridge, finished in 1591, was for more than two and a half centuries the only one to cross the Grand Canal (in 1854 the first Ponte dell'Accademia was constructed of iron). The twelve thousand poles of elm wood and the large number of planks of larch wood which hold it up, still support the only arch thirty metres wide with twenty-four shops which flank the ramps in groups of six on each side, and which divide the bridge into three ways, one in the centre with big steps and one on each side.

46

The XVI century church dedicated to San Giorgio, with its characteristic leaning Campanile is seen from the bridge of the Greeks: near is the School of the Greeks planned in 1678 by Baldassarre Longhena.

47.48.49

The Ca' d'Oro, one of the most exquisite jewels of Venetian Gothic art, erected by Marino Contarini, in the first decades of the XV century. The gilding which ornamented the facade — from which it derives its name — has disappeared. The inlaid polychrome marbles have remained intact and also the precious pattern of the six Gothic windows which veil the loggias, whose exquisite design was perhaps attributed to Marco d'Amadio, who was succeeded in the work of construction and decoration by the Lombard Marco Raverti and the Venetian Giovanni and Bartolomeo Bon. In 1896 Baron Giorgio Franchetti acquired the Ca' d'Oro and gathered there a rich collection of works of art, which was donated together with the Palace to the Italian State in 1916.

50.51

What mostly surprises the few careful observers of the Venetian bridges is the variety of their structures, true little works of art of ingenuity. Steps which go in two, three or even six directions (the bridge of the Bareteri, delle Mercerie); the extension of a bridge making room for the entrances to buildings, shops and inns; overhanging pavements start from them, four, five or even twenty metres long to steal a little bit of extra space to give another entrance to the houses which otherwise could only be entered from the canal. Dual bridges which cross with different arches two canals where they join. There exists at Santa Maria del Giglio even a bridge with half an arch which is an example like a hundred others, not of eccentricity, but of absolute convenience.

52.53

In every season of the year painters come from far away to enjoy themselves painting corners of Venice, choosing the hidden little squares, the quietest spots along the canals, a tiny bridge behind which rises a little palace adorned with flowers. These are not the followers of the great painters of Venice, in the XVIII century, such as Canaletto, Guardi, Carlevarijs who painted monumental scenes, but rather the modest heirs of the nineteenth-century provincialism of Giacomo Favretto, of Milesi.

54

The famous singular staircase of Palazzo Contarini dal Bovolo, the most superb example of an "entrance from the ground" of a Venetian Palace, erected in the last years of the XV century, probably by Giovanni Candi. "Bovolo", it is superfluous to say, means in Venetian dialect, snail-shell.

55

The little island called San Giovanni Laterano — shaped like a wedge which projects into the water with four bridges which seem to anchor it to the surrounding islands — is one of the smallest of the 116 which constitute the city (including the ten of the Giudecca), among which meander 176 little canals within an overall network of around 40 kilometres.

56.57.58

The wooden statue of the Virgin defeating the Devil, set at the corner of a house in the Frari district is the naive expression of popular devotion. The Madonna set in a Gothic arch which links the houses facing each other in the "calle del Paradiso", near the bridge of the same name (Paradise Bridge) is a refined low-relief of the beginning of the XV century.

59.60

One of the elements which distinguish the Venetian Gothic house from the Renaissance one is the staircase; in the courtyard of the former, it is a noble architectural element but exposed to weathering (as in Palazzo Soranzo-Val Axel at Santa Marina, among the last built in the old style, No 59), while the latter, that of the XVI century, is internal, wide, inventive (such as in Palazzo Pasqualigo-Giovannelli at San Felice, No 60).

61

The "sotoporteghi", those passages often long and dark which, penetrating into the body of the buildings, connecting two *calli* or a little canal and a little street, represent one of the necessary solutions to the overall problem of pedestrian movement imposed by the configuration of the city, one of the remedies for the scarcity of space.

62

If one wants to believe an ancient chronicle, in 1112 there came to Venice from the Morea, now the Peloponnese, the three Mastelli brothers, Rioba, Sandi and Afani, provided with considerable wealth, who "built their very honourable house near the bridge of the Moors, thus called because of the figures of the three above mentioned brothers which were sculpted in the corners of the building together with their names". Rioba, the most akward of the three figures in stone, dressed in Oriental garb, with a large cap on his head, represented for a long time the mask behind which the anonymous authors of jokes and satires used to hide, the Venetian twin of the Roman *Pasquino* and *Marforio*.

63

If one limits the number to those that are generally considered bridges in the strict sense, and includes also, paying homage to its fame, the Bridge of Sighs, and excludes those crossing the lagoon as being outside the urban area, one would conclude that there are in Venice 410 bridges, of which two are *private*, going directly from the outside into the building. To the total one has to add the seven internal bridges of the Arsenal and the Railway Station.

64

The "Porta da Terra" of the Arsenal — the most evident, visible and populous place of the military and shipbuilding industry which fed the trade and the wars of Venice, is a fake and a masterpiece of masquerading. The triumphal arch was erected in 1460, when the Serenissima for the first time in her history, turned her greatest efforts to the expansion on the mainland while the decline of her dominion on the sea began. The two winged victories were added in 1570, after the battle of Lepanto, where the Venetians paid a very high price for their victory which at the final count was damaging for Venice and from which she came out weakened. The terrace in front of the gate, with eight statues of mythological divinities was built in 1682, when the number of the *arsenalotti*, the shipbuilding workers, had fallen from 15,000 at the end of the XV century to 2,400. The two imposing lions at the sides of the terraces were brought to Venice from Athens in 1687 after the conquest of the Morea, the last vain victory of Venice. Behind the masks of the marble monuments, the Arsenal, "the heart of the Venetian State" began dismantling her shipyards: Venice, already in her decline, dressed herself up for her sunset.

65

The equestrian statue of the Great Commander, Bartolomeo Colleoni, from Bergamo, designed and mostly carried out by Verrocchio, erected in front of the Scuola Grande of St. Mark's, the splendid seat of the most powerful Venetian religious fraternities and the masterpiece of Mauro Codussi.

66.67.68.69

Almost two centuries passed between the beginning of the work and the consecration of the church of San Giovanni e Paolo (No 66). The building which was begun around the middle of the XIII century, probably under the direction of one of the Dominican friars of the convent nearby, rose majestically, second only in size and decoration to the Basilica of St. Mark. On the other hand, the Franciscan friars, the *frari* as they were popularly called, who used to celebrate Mass in a small church in another corner of the city, beyond the Grand Canal, moved perhaps by a spirit of emulation, jealousy and competion, began building themselves a similarly imposing church (No 69), in 1340, when the framework of the Dominican church was almost finished. The competition which ended in the first half of the XV century, did not produce a winner, resulting in the two churches being the most solemn examples of Gothic architecture in Venice. The church of San Giovanni e Paolo enjoyed, though, the privilege of housing the funerary monuments of the Doges and eminent people (Nos 67-68), becoming the Pantheon of the Serenissima.

70.71

On the journey to the island of the cemetery, where Diaghilev, Stravinsky and Ezra Pound wanted to be buried, one can see the city behind, on whose outline rise the *campanili* of a hundred churches.

72

Lurking about the *calli* and crossing the bridges with the ease of those who feel at home; idly curled up on a well in a little square or stretched out in the sun in a passageway with superior indifference; they appear at the window of the ground floor, curious or crouching. Where do those miriads of cats come from, that populate Venice? They show an ancient familiarity with the city. But where do they go to die? Independent, elegant, and mysterious to the last, they disappear no-one knows where, discreet, without leaving any physical trace, no smell of death. If they die at all.

73

The two ways of moving around the lagoon city and the footpaths — *le calli* (the little streets), *i sotoporteghi* (covered passageways), the bridges, *le fondamente* (the overhanging pavements) which flank the little canals, are a device where each element finds its own place, a puzzle which the Venetian beaver has organised with patient and ingenious work to bend the order and disorder of nature to his own needs.

74.75

The gondola (from the Greek *ondylion,* bowl?, from the Latin *cymbula,* a little boat?) born together with Venice, is a light boat suited to plough through the tricky shallow waters of the lagoon, developed and made perfect in time, under the imperious needs of necessity until it acquired its present purity of line. "It is a rigorous masterpiece of aestethics and naval science, of absolute stability on the water, with her graceful thrust of prow and stern completing the body, everything calculated for perfect balance" (G. Marangoni). Her traditional dimensions (10.835 metres long and a maximum width of 1 m. 42) have been respected for centuries. Her aspect has instead changed since, in a period of austerity, with a decree (the Sumptuary Laws) by the *Provveditori alle Pompe* dated April 1633, which banned any sort of furnishing or decoration which might manifest that luxury which the decadent city tried uselessly to restrain. The gondola divested herself of every colour and remained black but not funereal, on the contrary merry and light in her brightness.

76.77

In Campo San Beneto there rises a huge palace built by the Pesaro family in the XV century, which became famous, later on when it was the seat of a famous Society of Music called the *Apollinea,* as the *Palazzo degli Orfei.* The Spanish nobleman Mariano Fortuny y Madrazo, a passionate lover of Venice (where he died in 1950) acquired the ancient building and restored it to house there a rich and singular collection of fabrics, clothes and paintings whose central nucleus was made up of works by Fortuny himself, a versatile artist whose talent showed itself principally in the creation of exquisite fabrics. In 1956 his wife Henriette donated the Palace and the collections to the city.

78

Until a century ago the only drinkable water supply in Venice came from the rain collected in wells scattered about the city, in the little squares and private courtyards, of which remain the *vere,* the ornamental well-heads, to-day a characteristic ornament, once a true source of life.

79

Floating markets like that which surprises and cheers one along the bank of the little canal of San Barnaba, were once numerous around the city; coming from Mazzorbo, from Sant'Erasmo, from the Vignole — the islands cultivated as orchards — the boats carried fruit, vegetables, herbs for seasoning, to every quarter, for the women who leaned out over the *fondamenta*.

80

Very numerous are the little irregular bridges, even "crooked" as they are popularly called and sometimes also in the official toponomy. As a vital and widespread element of the city network of streets, the bridges were born after the alleyways, and it was necessary to build them obliquely across the canals, because they link two streets which come out on to the canal not opposite each other but as they were made, independently, before the need for bridges arose.

81

The miriad of little altars and tabernacles with images of the Virgin and of the Saints which you run into in every street — which here are called *capitelli* — bear witness to the intense religious fervour which has run through Venice throughout her intense history, but also are the discreet symbol of her pragmatism. Before the XVIII century, when street lighting was being extended all over the city, only the areas of San Marco and the Rialto were sufficiently well-lit by night, while all the little streets remained in complete darkness, broken only by weak lights in front of the sacred images of the *capitelli* at the street corners. It was Domenico Michiel who was Doge from 1118 to 1130, who ordered that the darkest little streets should be provided with *cesendoli* (from the Latin *cicendula*, firefly) by the parish priests, little lights sufficient at least to show the way on the darkest nights. We have no means of knowing whether the pious *capitelli* or the useful *cesendoli* were born first, but it is certain that once again the abstract principles found confirmation and sustenance for their practical convenience.

82

Light is like a wind
which runs across the green surface
of the canal, ruffling in with touches of silver,
Then it is engulfed in the shade and is lost.
(Diego Valeri, from *The Flute with Two Pipes*)

83.84.85.86.87.88.89.90.91.92

Festivals, ephemeral paradises, "bread and circuses, a mixture of nobility and populace, ladies and prostitutes" in an orgy of colours, elegance, flamboyant inventions, suggested by unleashed capricious fancy. Unleashed because masked. Overflowing joy or pretentiousness? Venice, a city of a two-faceted character re-invents masks for each Carnival: a Carnival which never ends, perpetuated by visitors (should we call them tourists? Or fleeting Sunday trippers? Or crowds of people curious about everything, resigned to the duty of having to visit Venice?) who look at the gilded masks in the shop windows — it is cardboard painted gold, a simulation which is doubled.
One knows that the merriment is over, but one stretches it out modelling other noses and cheeks exaggerated to excess, which is the grotesque, or at least, mere coyness, but fictitious all the same. Powders and other beauty aids, streamers and music are prepared for distraction, diversion and entertainment, to create two people out of one, in a city born with two faces, like the government which she gave herself — never absolute, never democratic, a compendium of oblique interests and restraints masked by delegation, as Giacomo Casanova well knew: "Well-governed as it seems to us, let us not complain that talking about the way we are governed has been forbidden, and let us believe ourselves much happier when well-provided for, without obligation to think of anything, than if we had to assume worries and at the same time we were granted freedom to talk about everything". This ambiguous personality, a lover through frustration, was breathing the last breaths of the gasping *Serenissima Repubblica* which was increasing the quantity of grease-paint in the process of the devastation of her face. Tragic or comic, devilish or divine, the mask continues in the revived Carnival to suggest a double identity. Is the sumptuousness of the costumes happiness or desolate aestheticism? Are they human creatures or are they mere dummies, the figures with, in the background, the ethereal Bridge of Sighs?

93.94.95.96.97

The Pageant of the Marine Republics and the Historical Regatta. The Doge invited his fellow Dukes of Amalfi, Genoa and Pisa; there is definitive and absolute peace between the dominating powers of the Mediterranean because the powerful Republics exist no longer, the princes are only actors, the ostentatious opulence is splendid simulation which is repeated every year in the lagoon and the Grand Canal, for the historical procession of coloured ghosts.

98

Some popular Venetian festivals, such as Carnival or the Feast of the Redeemer offer the atmospheric spectacle of fireworks against the night sky of the lagoon.

Giancarlo Gasponi

An encounter with Venice

Venice, the most photographic and, people say, the most photographed city in the world. A place of dreams, an invention, a fiction of the imagination where the incredible, the unlikely, emerges at every step, is concealed behind every corner. Perhaps no other reality like this, of such singular beauty that it cannot be compared to any other, has been represented at such length and in such variety, photographed, filmed, and reproduced in every way. In planning a book of photographs on Venice, my first impression was in fact that of finding myself opposite a reality already deeply inquired into, explored in every detail, and illustrated in every one of her aspects. I confess I had never before set foot in the city of the lagoon, though this could have been somehow an element in my favour. My first encounter with the Serenissima, with her overflowing creative vitality, the extraordinarily changeable character of this city, did away, however, with every fear of finding myself working with an image, already overworked and known to everyone. I went to Venice for the first time in February and when I arrived there it was already late evening. A gondola took me to the hotel, in Santo Stefano, gliding silently through dark and winding canals. With the hustle and bustle of the metropolis still in my head, and the continuous noise of the motorway, I was at once struck by that almost perfect silence accompanied only by the sound of the water and by soft voices which arose and almost immediately died away every time the gondola went under a bridge. (I gradually became accustomed to that quiet, to that slow-paced and contemplative rhythm which Venice acquires during the cold months, when she is not being invaded by hoards of tourists, so that I returned with great vexation to the usual movement, hectic and mechanical, of life in the big cities). Suddenly there opened out in front of me a wide surface of water crossed by other boats, over which loomed the dark facades of palaces which looked like the wings in a theatre without depth. It had to be the Grand Canal. The gondola cut across it obliquely to immerse herself once more in the intricate network of little canals. The weak lights coming from the alleyways cast patches of light on an indefinite landscape producing reflections, half-lights, appearances and illusions. The succession of glimpses, of corners, of singular light effects which attracted my attention was so crowded that I was stupefied by it. Mentally I was already taking photographs. No film could ever have been able to penetrate that darkness. As soon as I arrived, Venice threw her magic in my face without even giving me time to take breath. And almost without appearing herself. In the semi-darkeness of the canals I reached the hotel without in fact having been able to distinguish anything clearly. But in the silence of that dark labyrinth I had felt the city surrounding me as though it were a vivid presence full of magic vibrations. Thus in the crowd of indistinct expectations, which this singular approach aroused, the thought of to-morrow filled me with subtle excitment.

The following morning Venice seemed to have decided not to show herself, at least distinctly. A dense fog, like those which frequently cover the lagoon in the winter season, made it impossible to see even a few metres ahead. Was this the "ghost city, unreal and melancholic", "a landscape of death" seen in so many works of art pervaded by a complacent, decadent fantasy? Strangely enough, yet perhaps not so strangely, this aspect of Venice could not arouse in me any sense of sadness. On the contrary, this very fog, full of mysterious light, gave to the landscape a certain fascination. Everything became blurred, ambiguous, untouchable. The sky, blended with the water, the light with the colours, reality with fiction. Faded into this luminous vapour, the architecture seemed to be born out of the water and to flow into the sky in a single evanescent substance. As though immersed in an amniotic fluid, Venice evoked the idea of a mythical origin, of a remote and eerie event, and of a creature of the lagoon.

With difficulty, caused by the poor visibility, I reached St. Mark's. From the vast area of the piazza, enclosed by fog, there emerged all of a sudden and then immediately faded into the indefinite grey, the elegant shape of the *Procuratie*, the heavy mass of the *Campanile*, the orientalising outline of Saint Mark's. I decided to enter the church where I stayed a long time looking in the semi-darkness for the golden mosaics, visiting the Treasure, and admiring the famous horses. When, after spending nearly two hours there, I reappeared in the square, I was immediately hit in the face by an unexpected glow. A very limpid light vibrated in the clear and tepid air. Thousands of pigeons crowded together on the stone slabs forming black spots on the handfuls of grain thrown by tourists, while people coming from the shade of the arcades crossing past each other, seemed to have a pleased and amused air about them. Shops and bars had opened, animating the long galleries where resounded the ringing voices of school children visiting the city. Finally, I was actually seeing Venice! I remained stunned by how this city could change her aspect so quickly, creating a spell, different each time, almost as though she were bewitched. Once the vapour of the lagoon was dissolved, here was a landscape clear and lively, a gentle and caressing atmosphere, which created a sparkling mood, ready for any discovery. And here there is no lack of discoveries to be made, so many as to take your breath away.

Whoever is sensitive to beauty or art, or possesses at least a good dose of curiosity, finding himself suddenly at St. Mark's, could be disconcerted for a moment. So great is the crowding of images which forcibly attract one's attention so as to kindle a feverish activity of the senses, a frenzied attempt to absorb every vision, every suggestion offered, that one can be overwhelmed by it. One must keep calm, take a deep breath and organize one's thoughts. But it is difficult to follow a plan: it is impossible then, for a photographer. The rational and methodical reporter will see his ordered plan of work disintegrate at the first approach, finding himself trying to catch the city herself in her capricious changes. Every pre-arranged itinerary is furthermore strewn with such a variety and so many elements of attraction, as to be fragmented into a hundred episodes, a hundred discoveries, and a hundred unforeseeable encounters. What disorientates the photographer is the infinite possibilities of angles for every photograph, each one different, each one interesting and original. Accustomed to frame in the viewfinder what constitutes the main interest, leaving out that which is of lesser value, here one finds the impossibility of turning one's back on anything insignificant. That which attracts follows on without interruption: it is a peculiarity of the city of the Doges.

But it is not only the exceptional concentration of monuments and works of art which stimulated the feverish desire to take pictures in those who, photographers or tourists, wander about the stones of Venice with a sensitive and enchanted soul. Here aesthetic and poetical values are brought to life as nowhere else. And one is not surprised to find oneself photographing the ruin of a palace covered with moss or the gnawed shape of a crumbling doorway, when also the sumptuous decadence of the buildings, among the last sparkles of an aristocratic splendour, becomes an element of lyrical impression. The stimuli, the opportunities for finding a shot are the most varied. The most usual sight offers a starting point for the most sophisticated compositions... the gondola, that most elegant graphic line, where the eye of the photographer lingers at length, attracted by the most extraordinary singularity of its shape. A shape perfectly completed which could not have been imagined, only discovered.

For photographing Venice the best seasons are certainly winter and spring. In the summer everything appears flat and blinding, and also the air is oppressive, made heavy by the sirocco. On some winter days everything seems, instead, to contribute to a miracle. It is enough to go down the Grand Canal in the early morning. A light, mellow and golden, multiplied and echoed by the water, falls sideways on the elegant forms of the palaces, exalting the richness of the facades, enhancing the precious embroidery of the decorations. With the passing of the hours the magic penetrates into the intricate network of the waterways, repeating itself in every little canal, every little street, every little square. In January or February, it might snow, and no landscape is so fairy-like under its white mantle.

However, so much fascination, so much originality, can be the undoing of a photographer. The major danger, always ready to strike, is that of losing oneself in the commonplace, ending up by sticking respectfully to those conventional pictures of Venice diffused by the mass-media, whose proven capacity to amaze is regularly exploited in the programmes of the great tourist machine. Here is the danger that the unusual may become obvious, or better, that the unusual as such, becomes obvious. As a reaction against this, it may happen that one suddenly discovers one's own strong iconoclastic vocation and gives into the fascination of the easy transgression, at times too pert, too gratuitous, too much taken for granted. Perhaps to comprehend the authentic dimension of this city, the only thing left to do is to let oneself go as fully as possible within her, to assimilate her rhythms, her moods, her innermost breathing. The ideal would be to fall in love with Venice. And it is certainly not difficult. One would gain thus, in one's work, that total dedication and that passion that sweeps away in one puff the shining patina of the commonplace, to catch the intimate life of things. Certainly, it is necessary to preserve a good dose of detachment to make oneself critical and selective in taking photographs, but secretly, without others seeing it, pretending you are doing nothing. It is preferable with Venice, to hide one's own possessive anxiety behind the candour of an ecstatic admiration.

Technical Note

I cannot report the list of technical data relative to each picture, as recently has been the case in some photographic publications. I am not accustomed to annotating them and I could not recall them all exactly. For those who are very keen on photographic techniques, I can only say that I have used two Nikon bodies (F3 and FE2), together with lenses with a focal length ranging from 20 to 200mm. Rarely did I use a teleconverter, while I did make use of a steady tripod whenever I could. The combination of Kodachrome 25 ASA and the tripod, is the best method of guaranteeing incisiveness and the absence of grain necessary to the enlarging of pictures to the size of the book. I have never made use of coloured filters, neither had recourse to tricks of any kind. They are not necessary. Whoever goes to the lagoon during the winter months, with a little patience and a little bit of good luck, will find, on certain days, maybe towards dawn or sunset, the atmosphere full of the colour of some of the pictures in this book.

By the same author:

Rome Revealed Editoria - Trento

Rome Water and Stone Editoria - Trento

Rome A special journey Editoria - Trento

Splendid Florence Editoria - Trento

Portrait of Rome Editoria - Trento

Glorious Cities Editoria - Trento

Carnival in Venice Editoria - Trento

Graphics and layout:
Giancarlo Gasponi - Rouhyeh Avaregan.

The author wishes to thank Fahim Avaregan
and Graziella Sereni for their
valuable suggestions in the
arrangement of the layout.

Photolithography: Zincografia Verona
Phototypesetting: GI Grafica Internazionale - Rome
Printed by Printers s.r.l. - Trento July 1986